REBELS
RESCUED

Brian Cosby has written a wonderful little book—simple, clear, and deep all at once—setting forth the essentials of Reformed theology. A helpful primer for students, and for anyone else who has ever wondered, "What's all this fuss about?"

TIMOTHY GEORGE,
*Founding Dean of Beeson Divinity School and general editor
of the Reformation Commentary on Scripture*

Brian Cosby has a heart to communicate God's truth to students in an honest straightforward manner. *Rebels Rescued* takes the great truths of the Reformed Faith and presents them in an accessible, easy to read, and concise way. This book will be a tremendous resource for churches and families seeking to disciple and equip the next generation of laborers for the Kingdom of God.

BRAD WALLER,
*Associate Pastor of Youth and Families at the Independent
Presbyterian Church, Savannah, Georgia, Youth pastor in the PCA*

Without blurring the beauty of or shallowing the depth of Reformed theolgy, Brian Cosby in *Rebels Rescued* has been able to write a book that makes the truth of our theological heritage accessible to young minds. Packed with timely illustrations, key scriptures and important historical facts from the Reformation, this primer has more than enough information for the student who wants to know more about Reformed theology. No longer will I struggle to recommend a resource when I am asked about a clear way to explain Reformed theology to students ... *Rebels Rescued* will not only be the first but I suspect the only book I will need to recommend from this point forward!

DANNY MITCHELL,
Coordinator of Youth and Families, Presbyterian Church in America

Rebels Rescued turns to the beautiful old truths of the Reformation and perfectly targets them at a whole new generation. As a Reformed theology primer it is a joy to read.

TIM CHALLIES
Pastor and Blogger

REBELS
RESCUED

A STUDENT'S GUIDE TO
REFORMED THEOLOGY

BRIAN H. COSBY

CF4·K

10 9 8 7 6 5 4 3 2
Copyright © 2012 Brian H. Cosby
Reprinted in 2018
paperback ISBN 978-1-5271-0238-5
epub ISBN 978-1-78191-085-6
mobi ISBN 978-1-78191-086-3

Previously printed in 2012
ISBN 978-1-84550-980-4

Published
by
Christian Focus Publications,
Geanies House, Fearn, Tain,
Ross-shire, IV20 1TW, U.K.

Cover design by Paul Lewis

Printed and bound by
Bell and Bain, Glasgow

MIX
Paper from
responsible sources
FSC® C007785
www.fsc.org

Scripture quotations are from The Holy Bible,
English Standard Version, copyright © 2001 by
Crossway Bibles, a division of Good News Publishers.
Used by permission. All rights reserved.

"Hymn to a Gracious Sovereign" © 2005
by Neil Barham. Used by permission.

To

Dad & Dianne

with thankfulness for their basement
collection of Reformed theology

CONTENTS

WHAT IS REFORMED THEOLOGY?

Shouting "I'm a Calvinist!" can get you in big trouble. At least it did for me. My classmates looked at me as if I were from the planet "Narrow-minded"—or worse! The teacher scowled, my peers glared and my face transitioned from one shade of red to another.

John Calvin (1509-1564) was a principal leader of the Protestant Reformation, a movement in sixteenth-century Europe that initially sought to reform the Roman Catholic Church back to a Christ-exalting, gospel-believing, and Word-centered expression of the Christian faith. However, the leadership of the Church had no intention of reform.

The cries for reform, however, didn't begin in the sixteenth century. Many clergy were corrupt—living luxurious lives of rampant immorality and sexual promiscuity. Church positions were given to the highest bidder or to family members and widespread skepticism plagued the church due to its moral bankruptcy.

In addition to this, the church had created a theology apart from the Bible that sought to keep certain structures in place. For example, at the beginning of the sixteenth century, the Pope plunged headfirst into a building campaign to raise money for St. Peter's in Rome. In order to fund his endeavors, he revived and extended the practice of selling indulgences.

For a sum of money, you could waive your time in purgatory or even have one of your dead relatives immediately go to heaven. By buying one of these indulgences or doing various works of penance, a person could earn his way into God's favor. Salvation less and less became about something God does and more and more about something man earns by works.

A young German monk, named Martin Luther (1483-1546), responded to the various moral abuses of the church and of a "salvation by works" theology by nailing ninety-five theses—

statements of faith—to the church door in Wittenberg. Thanks to the printing press (invented around 1450), these theses were quickly printed and distributed across Germany. The Protestant Reformation had begun.

Reformed theology, as we have come to call it, is first and foremost biblical theology—the study and discourse on the character and work of God as revealed in the Bible. Thus, this book is about God, his glorious character and his work of salvation.

We can summarize Reformed theology by ten expressions. The first five are what is often called the "Five Solas"—referring to the Latin word for "only" or "alone." The second five are organized by the acrostic, TULIP, or what has been called the "Five Points of Calvinism." The first five may also be applied generally to evangelical Christians while the second five are more specific to Reformed Christians. These ten expressions, then, are:

1. *Sola Scriptura* – the Bible alone is the only source of authority for faith, doctrine and Christian living.

2. *Sola Fide* – We are justified—declared "righteous" before God by faith alone, and not by works.

3. *Sola Gratia* – We are saved by God's grace alone, shown in the glorious gospel of Jesus Christ and applied by the Holy Spirit.

4. *Solus Christus* – There is salvation in no one else but Jesus Christ, the only mediator between God and man.

5. *Soli Deo Gloria* – All glory and honor is due to God alone and to no other.

6. *Total Depravity* – Man, because of his sinful nature, is born into this world dead in sin, enslaved to its services and inclined toward evil continually.

7. *Unconditional Election* – God's sovereign choice of his people from before the foundation of the world is not dependent upon man's decision or will, but upon God's free grace.

8. *Limited Atonement* – Christ came to purposefully and intentionally die for God's elect, his people.

9. *Irresistible Grace* – God, by his Spirit, effectually calls and saves sinners by grace.

10. *Perseverance of the Saints* – Once a person is saved, he or she will always be saved; true salvation cannot be lost.

This book is an introduction to Reformed theology with a particular view towards teenagers. In such a small-print world, where everything comes with a disclaimer and small print, this book is meant to be a straightforward discussion and investigation of these ten expressions of Reformed thought, summarized into eight short chapters.

Each chapter is broken down into helpful segments and includes a "Reflection Questions" section for individual or group study. It is the author's hope that you will be more informed, encouraged and even challenged as you explore the tenets of Reformed theology.

REBELS AT HEART

I love grocery-store shopping carts. Even as a kid, I loved following my mother around the store while she tossed in the bread, milk and—if I was good—cookies! But shopping carts often have a serious flaw. Have you ever had one with a bad wheel? You try to push it around and all it wants to do is run into the sides of the aisle. If you were to let it go on its own, it would immediately turn and smash into that case of pickles up ahead!

Your heart is very similar. You are the shopping cart and the bad wheel is your heart. It's always veering off, leading us away from what we were originally created to be. We were created to roll through life, bearing the fruit of God's love and glory, but instead, every one of us has a heart that deceitfully pulls us away from following Jesus and into something much worse than a case of pickles.

ONE MESSED-UP WORLD!

You have most likely had at least a couple of history courses in school— maybe a history of the world and a history of your own country. In the United States, there's little history— being a nation that's only a couple hundred years old!

But even in that relatively short time, there have been two world wars, conflicts that have changed the world map, and the rise of global terrorism. In fact, these last two have probably taken place within your own lifetime. Graphic pictures of these conflicts find their way onto the Internet and the rest, as they say, is history. We live in one messed-up world.

But have you ever asked, "Why is this world so messed up? Why are our hearts prone to swerve toward evil like that shopping cart toward the pickles? Why do we get angry, even with friends? Why if you ask a two-year-old not to touch wet paint, he immediately begins drawing pictures in it? Are we taught to disobey or does that come naturally?"

SPIRITUALLY DEAD

Remember that Reformed theology is first and foremost biblical theology. In other words, the elements of Reformed theology come straight from God's Word, the Bible. The first point about Reformed theology is that we are rebels at heart. This is often called, in Reformed theology, "total depravity." Without God's grace performing a divine heart transplant, everything in us seeks to rebel against God. But why are we rebels at heart?

God tells us in the book of Ephesians that—before he saved you—"you were dead in the trespasses and sins in which you once walked" (Ephesians 2:1-2). It's a humbling thought that we were born into this world spiritually dead. Unless you're dreaming, dead people don't walk. They don't talk. They can't do anything— they're dead! If you were to take a spoonful of life-giving medicine up to the lips of a dead person, would he or she take it and drink it? No, because, well ... you get the idea.

This is an important point to consider. Even from birth, we are dead in sin

(Psalm 51:5). As a physically dead person cannot do anything that is physically productive, a spiritually dead person cannot do anything that is spiritually good. Being spiritually dead means that we are unable to respond to anything good. The issue is not freedom to do something, but ability.

I remember raising my hand and asking my first-grade teacher: "Can I use the restroom?" She replied: "I'm sure you can, but may you?" She was differentiating between having ability and having freedom, which are two different things. A fish, for example, has the freedom to fly—if it even had the desire—but not the ability.

Being a rebel at heart means that we do not have the ability to choose God or even to respond to God on our own because we are spiritually dead. The reason that you and I are spiritually dead from birth is that our first parents—Adam and Eve—disobeyed God in the Garden of Eden (Genesis 3). You might ask, "Why am I spiritually dead because of something they did?" Great question.

REBEL IN PARADISE

God created Adam and Eve and placed them in a beautiful garden. They were to live and enjoy constant and perfect fellowship with God. God gave them only one command in this garden. While they could enjoy all of the benefits of living there, they were not allowed to eat of the tree of the knowledge of good and evil (Genesis 2:17). The result of breaking this command, they were told, was death. But, by the tempting of Satan in the form of a serpent, they ate of the tree and that fellowship with God was broken. As a result, they were barred from the "tree of life" and death entered the world (Genesis 3:22). The image of God in which man was created, though not lost, was shattered.

As the first man in this world, the Bible tells us that Adam was our representative. He represented all of his offspring, which includes you and me and the rest of humanity. Whatever he did would be true for all those whom he represented. Whatever decisions he made affected all those who would follow after him.

I grew up playing soccer or, as it's called in the rest of the world, football. Before the games would begin, our team would send the captain to the middle of the field to meet a player from the opposing team, together with the referee. The referee would flip a coin and the players would call "heads" or "tails" to decide who started with possession of the ball. The captain was our representative. He made a decision on behalf of the team. In other words, his decision affected the condition of the game and his team's players.

Because Adam represented all of humanity, his decision would affect the condition of this world and all its inhabitants. The guilt of his sin and rebellion against God has been placed upon the team of humanity. That is why the effects of sin—cancer, disease, war, anger, lust, death, and even the thorns on bushes—have been a reality ever since. "Just as sin came into the world through one man, and death through sin," the apostle Paul writes, "so death spread to all men because all sinned" (Romans 5:12). That first rebellion in paradise has become the rebellion in your heart and in my heart.

DUPED BY SMALL JOY

Have you ever had someone tell an ugly lie about you to others? It doesn't feel good. That's because lies hurt. God's Word tells us that "the heart is deceitful above all things, and desperately sick" (Jeremiah 17:9). This means that our hearts tell us lies. The things you often feel will satisfy and bring you ultimate happiness are probably the things that will bring you greatest despair and loneliness when they fail to deliver that promise.

International speaker and author, Ravi Zacharias, once said, "The loneliest moment in life is when you have just experienced that which you thought would deliver the ultimate, and it has let you down." Our hearts deceive us into thinking that the things of this world will bring great joy, only to be duped. Enjoying the pleasures of this world offer small joy—and oftentimes fake joy—compared to the enjoyment and satisfaction found in God. The truth is—to quote C. S. Lewis:

"If we consider the unblushing promises of reward and the staggering nature of the rewards promised in the Gospels, it would seem that Our Lord

finds our desires not too strong, but too weak. We are half-hearted creatures, fooling about with drink and sex and ambition when infinite joy is offered us, like an ignorant child who wants to go on making mud pies on a slum because he cannot imagine what is meant by the offer of a holiday at the sea. We are far too easily pleased."

Being a rebel at heart means that, because our hearts are deceitful, we trade true and grand joy for "mud pies." Even after God by his grace saves us, we continue to rebel against him and his goodness.

If you are a Christian, you will have days when you feel close to God and days when you don't. This is "normal", although not "normal" in the way that you and I were originally created to be. You may feel that you are on a roller coaster of faith, wondering if there's a loop up ahead—and afraid of derailing! The amazing promise of God, however, is that once you have been set on the track of faith, God will never let you derail. You are held by a sovereign love that won't let you go!

Even though grace has dealt the deathblow to the dragon of your rebellious heart, that dragon continues to lash out like a wounded animal. While you might feel as though this roller coaster of faith is leading nowhere at times, God's grace is continually carrying you towards your heavenly home.

A RE-FORMED HEART

There is a fundamental difference between the idea that we are sinners *because* we sin and the idea that we sin *because* we are sinners. Read that line again. The first idea—that we are sinners because we sin—puts our outward sin as the reason that we are called sinners. However, Reformed theology teaches us that this second idea is actually the truer statement: we sin because we are sinners. Or, to put it another way, we rebel because we are rebellious by nature. Out of our rebellious hearts comes rebellion.

After Adam sinned in the Garden of Eden, sin spread like wildfire among his children and their children, until it seemed like the whole of humanity was in the grips of rebellion. Genesis 6:5 explains, "The LORD saw that the wickedness of man was great in the earth, and that every intention of the thoughts of his heart was only evil continually." Sin goes deeper than the outward anger, violence, and gossip that we commit day by day. It lies hidden in the intentions of the heart.

Many students that I know struggle—as I do—with doing nice things for people with the wrong motive. When I was sixteen years old, an elderly lady in my church (who also happened to be very wealthy) asked me to do her a favor. She wanted me to come to clean her windows. At once, I was confronted by the evil intention of my heart. Would I clean her windows because the gospel of grace compelled me to, or was it because I wanted her money? I confess that I cleaned her windows because I wanted her money. I made sure she saw how hard I was working. When I finished, she told me how grateful she was and that she would see me on Sunday. With that, I left—with an angry heart! I felt like I deserved her money and, when she didn't give, my rebellious heart welled up within me.

GETTING WHAT WE DESERVE

God's Word teaches that our rebellion has consequences. Romans 3:23 states, "For the wages of sin is death." The consequence of sin, therefore, is death. But what about the little sins? Do those deserve death too? This is important. All sin—as the Bible teaches—is rebellion against God. Moreover, realizing that we are rebels at heart and not rebels because we rebel, we see how deep the sin of our hearts really goes. It deserves death and hell.

This, understandably, is not popular today. We hear all the time that we deserve a new car or a new bike or whatever is the latest and greatest. But the picture we get from Scripture is that, because of our deep-seated sin, we actually deserve death and hell. These are the "wages" of our rebellious hearts.

On it's own, your rebellious heart has no hope. You're dead in sin, following the emptiness of this world as you struggle with a heart that is only "evil continuously." BUT GOD— two of the greatest words in the Bible (cf. Ephesians 2:4)—takes our cold, rebellious heart of stone and gives us a new heart that is re-formed for his glory and our joy. This is God's promise: "I will give you a new heart" (Ezekiel 36:26).

Reformed theology teaches that, because we are more sinful than we could ever imagine, it can only be God who does a work of grace in giving us a new heart. He takes that broken wheel and replaces it with one that has both the ability and the desire to seek him and to follow him. By faith in Christ, you are no longer set on a trajectory that smashes into the aisles of sinful destruction. No, his promises beckon us onward as he carries us in his grip of grace.

REFLECTION QUESTIONS

- What sins do you continually struggle with—veering you off course away from a closer relationship with Jesus?

- Are you sometimes deceived by your own heart? Do you sometimes fall into the trap of thinking something will bring you joy and satisfaction only to be "let down" when it doesn't?

- As Adam is the representative head for those who belong to him, how might Jesus be the representative Head for those who belong to him? Read Romans 5:12-19.

- Why is it difficult to believe that our sin actually deserves death and hell?

ELECTED BY LOVE

Calvinism: *The Group that Chooses You*, was the name of the Facebook group. I clicked it and, ironically, it was I who chose to join. I've seen the same slogan on T-shirts and bumper stickers. What's interesting is that if you mention the name "John Calvin" or the word "predestination" in class, your classmates will probably begin casting apples in your direction! In the least, they will either look at you with a threatening glare or a sense of mystified wonder. Why do people get offended at the name John Calvin and the word predestination?

PREDESTINATION IN THE BIBLE

Reformed theology teaches from Scripture that, before God created the heavens and the earth, he has chosen—or "predestined"—his people to be saved for eternity. Consider some of these passages from the Bible:

- "Even as [God] chose us in [Christ] before the foundation of the world, that we should be holy and blameless before him. In love he predestined us for adoption as sons through Jesus Christ, according to the purpose of his will" (Ephesians 1:4-5).

- "For those whom [God] foreknew he also predestined to be conformed to the image of his Son" (Romans 8:29).

- "In [Christ] we have obtained an inheritance, having been predestined according to the purpose of him who works all things according to the counsel of his will" (Ephesians 1:11).

- "The LORD your God has chosen you to be a people for his treasured possession, out of all the peoples who are on the face of the earth" (Deuteronomy 7:6).

- "For we know, brothers loved by God, that he has chosen you" (1 Thessalonians 1:4).

"Predestination," therefore, is a biblical word; it comes straight from the Bible. Taken literally, it means to destine beforehand or to decisively determine something before it takes place. In the original Greek language, it is actually two words joined together (*pro-oridzo*). Many times, self-professing Christians will say, "I don't believe in predestination." While I understand their point—that they disagree with an interpretation of it—to say that they don't believe in it is contrary to the fact that it is in the Bible.

The biblical writers consistently use the words "elect," "election," "chosen," and "predestined." However it's stated, the message is clear: God has chosen his people before the foundation of the world for eternal salvation. Conversely, the non-Christian, "whose name has not been written before the foundation of the world in the book of life of the Lamb who was slain" (Revelation 13:8) "will go away into eternal punishment" (Matthew 25:46). Let's briefly look at this second point.

There is no doubt that the scriptural truth that non-Christians will go to hell is under attack in our day. There have been numerous books published in recent times re-affirming the reality and existence of hell precisely because of this attack. However, many people want to believe that if you are generally a "good person," you will go to heaven. You probably even hear this in your school or from your friends. But this isn't what Scripture teaches. Even Jesus speaks more about hell—and unbelievers going there—than any other person in the Bible!

Deep down, however, all of us want to know what is true, even if it's difficult to bear. You have been told too many lies to simply want what's easy. We live in a small-print world where everything comes with a disclaimer. Get a free computer (plus an arm and a leg if you qualify and can run a mile in thirty seconds!). From famous politicians to well-known preachers, we have witnessed the scandals and the hypocritical lives of prominent people. Because of this, we have been trained to be skeptics about what people say—especially if it sounds "too good to be true."

One of the common objections to predestination is: "If God has already elected those who will be saved, then why evangelize?" It's a good question and there are at least two primary reasons. First, we share the gospel because Jesus commands us to (Matthew 28:19).

Second, we share the gospel because it is the means by which God saves his elect—through the hearing of the preached word (Romans 10:17).

This second point is important. In the book of Acts, Luke records the apostle Paul and Barnabas preaching the gospel. He writes, "When the Gentiles heard [the gospel], they began rejoicing and glorifying the word of the Lord, and as many as were appointed to eternal life believed" (Acts 13:48). Did you catch that last line? Paul and Barnabas preached; the Lord saved. This is by God's design.

In such a small-print world, it's refreshing to let the Bible speak for itself. Yes, it is full of difficult doctrines, but would we expect anything less? If it always pleased our itching ears, we would see its shallowness and emptiness from the get-go.

But what we find in Scripture is so much more exciting and awe inspiring than small-print disclaimers. We are confronted with a God who calls his creation to worship him in spirit and in truth (John 4:24), to reflect back to him the radiance of his glory and to join in the chorus of the millennia of saints and of angels in heaven crying out, "Holy, holy, holy, is the Lord God Almighty!" This is the God we worship and adore. This is the God who reigns forever as the sovereign Creator over the universe. This is the God who elects his people by love.

PREDESTINATION AND CALVIN

So who was John Calvin and why do people get offended at him? As a sixteenth-century Reformer in Europe, John Calvin (1509-1564) sought to steer the church away from a man-centered view of the Christian faith to a God-centered view. In doing this, he emphasized God's absolute control over all things, a doctrine called God's sovereignty. There is neither one square inch nor one single molecule that is outside of God's control. God has "declared the end from the beginning," saying, "I have spoken, and I will bring it to pass; I have purposed, and I will do it" (Isaiah 46:11). The Psalmist writes, "For he spoke, and it came to be; he commanded, and it stood firm" (Psalm 33:9).

In asserting that God is in absolute control, the Bible teaches—and Calvin from the Bible—that we aren't. This doesn't mean, however, that we are mere robots or puppets. Man is fully responsible, while God is fully sovereign. In fact, the apostle Paul writes of both of these truths at the same time: "Work out your own salvation with fear and trembling [man's responsibility], for it is God who works in you, both to will and to work for his good pleasure [God's sovereignty]" (Philippians 2:12-13). Or consider this verse in Proverbs: "The heart of man plans his way, but the LORD establishes his steps" (Proverbs 16:9).

That God is sovereign, however, still offends. Why? Because we are rebels at heart. We want to be like God, like Satan's temptation in the Garden of Eden (Genesis 3:5). Submitting ourselves to greater wisdom, power, and holiness takes humility—something we rebels rebel against!

Because Calvin seemed to take freedom away from man, Calvin has been given a bad rap. But what Calvin sought to do, however, was to show that man's heart is not free to begin with. Our hearts are prone to wander away from Christ every time—if left on our own. Apart from God's grace in giving us new hearts to love him, we remain chained and imprisoned by sin and unbelief. There is no freedom apart from God's work of grace and it's grace precisely because his salvation is something we don't deserve.

WHAT IS "FAIR"?

Let's pretend for a moment that you, as a student, had one million pounds sterling (about 1.65 million U.S. dollars). You had mowed neighbors' yards or babysat their kids, and they were very generous people! Nevertheless, you earned that money. It was yours. You find yourself out walking one day and see an elderly homeless man digging through a dumpster. You have compassion on the man and so you decide to give him a hundred pounds. He didn't ask you, but you gave anyway. Unbeknownst to you, somebody down the street sees you and comes running up to you demanding that you give him one hundred pounds as well.

Stop. Think. Are you obligated to give this second man the money? Is he entitled to it? Absolutely not. But because of your generosity, there is a false sense of injustice—a false sense of thinking that you're not being fair to the second man.

When we begin considering God's eternal election of his people, before the foundation of the world, we must step back and ask the question: "What is fair?" Is it fair that everyone goes to heaven? Is God obligated to send everyone to heaven? Remember–the wages of sin is death and hell forever (cf. Romans 6:23). If we are all sinners, which we are, then the payment or the consequence of our sin is death and hell.

Therefore, in answer to our question, it would only be fair to send everybody to hell. The fact that God elects some people for salvation points to his grace and love. That God doesn't elect others points to his holiness and justice. Or to put it another way: by choosing some, he demonstrates his perfect love and grace. By not choosing others, he demonstrates his perfect holiness and justice. He is not obligated to save anybody. But because he wanted to demonstrate the greatness of his mercy, he poured out his grace upon the beloved bride of Christ, the church.

A COMFORTING THOUGHT

Think about this: If you were morally able to choose God apart from his grace and, therefore, enter into a saving relationship with him, then you could just as easily "unfriend" him and exit that saving relationship. The conditional element is you and your faith, not God. It would depend on how much you had a sense of faith or how much you felt like loving God. If you were strong in your faith one day, then you were saved. On the other hand, if you happen to have weak faith, then you would be unsaved.

But thank God that he is not in the business of non-committal, semi-secure summer friends, but of a sovereign, eternal, covenantal, loving, and grace-driven relationship with his people. The good news of the gospel is that your salvation isn't dependent upon you, but upon God's eternal electing love. If it was dependent upon you, you would never be saved to begin with because your heart would always choose evil every time—chained by sin and oriented toward sin, like that broken shopping-cart wheel.

Reformed theology points to this biblical truth: that before you were born, God set his love on you (Jeremiah 1:5). He chose you from before the foundation of the world to be his adopted child by his power and grace (Romans 9:10-23)—that he might "rejoice over you with gladness" and "quiet you by his love" (Zephaniah 3:17). If you know yourself this day to be a believer in Christ, you can take great comfort that you have been elected by a sovereign love that won't let you go.

 ## REFLECTION QUESTIONS

- Have you been offended by predestination? Have you experienced others being offended? What offended you/them most?

- Is the truth about hell difficult to believe? Why is this idea being attacked in our culture today?

- How might you explain, in your own words, the idea of election or predestination?

- How might God being absolutely sovereign over all things bring you comfort? What about during difficult times of suffering or when you feel that you have weak faith?

- How is it that Christians are elected by love?

FOR HIS SHEEP

One of my favorite board games is Monopoly. I'm not very good at it and I usually don't win. But I like it because of the thrill of having my opponent land on my property—and then searching to see how much "rent" he or she owes me. If you are familiar with the game, you know that "Boardwalk" or if you're in the U.K. "Mayfair" is the game's most highly valued property. If you own one of these, and your opponent lands on it during their turn, they will pay a nice sum of money—especially if you have put up houses or a hotel.

Recently, I was playing Monopoly and had purchased Boardwalk. I was excited because I'm usually never able to buy it. But to my disappointment, my opponent never landed on Boardwalk the entire game, even though I had put up a hotel on it! I had purchased it, paid for it, and put everything I had into that property, but my opponent never landed on it. It was a risk that I took and a risk that I lost.

DOES GOD TAKE RISKS?

Like my experience with Monopoly, some self-proclaiming Christians believe that God took a big risk in sending his Son to die on the cross. At great cost to himself, Jesus died in hopes that people in this world would land on the "Boardwalk of faith" and believe. But, from God's point of view, there was no guarantee. God put everything he had—his only Son—into extending the offer of salvation to lost sinners and took a risk in hopes that somebody might believe.

Other Christians believe that Jesus died for all people everywhere, and not just for the elect. This belief is called "universal atonement." Christ's sacrifice of atonement on the cross was for the entire human population throughout all time. This belief, also, is rather risky. It contends that Christ extends the hand of salvation to all of humanity, pleading that people might grab on by faith. This belief places salvation completely in their lap, not God's. While Christ's sacrificial death on the cross certainly covers Christians, the rest of the atonement—the atonement for all non-Christians—goes to waste. It is, as it were, ineffective and purposeless.

The other interesting element about this last view is that, if Jesus really died for everyone, then everyone would go to heaven. In other words, if Christ died for the unbeliever, then that unbeliever would not go to hell. Why? Because his sins have been atoned for!

INTENTIONAL ATONEMENT

Opposed to these two views, Reformed theology teaches that Christ was born into this world to die for his people, his sheep. Historically Reformed theology has been called "Limited Atonement"—not limited in the sense that Christ's atoning sacrifice is lacking, but because his death on the cross was intended only for God's elect. Or, to put it another way, Christ's death on the cross was intentional, purposeful, and definite only for those who would believe.

Jesus did not come to die for the unbeliever, but for his people, chosen before the foundation of the world.

Jesus said, "I am the good shepherd. The good shepherd lays down his life for the sheep" (John 10:11). He adds: "I am the good shepherd. I know my own and my own know me...and I lay down my life for the sheep" (v. 14). The apostle Paul explains this idea in context of husbands and wives. He writes, "Husbands, love your wives, as Christ loved the church and gave himself up for her" (Ephesians 5:25). Jesus died only for those whose names have been "written before the foundation of the world in the book of life of the Lamb who was slain" (Revelation 13:8).

Reformed theology teaches that Christ gave up his life to purchase the Boardwalk of faith for those whom he not only knew would land on it but also those whom he chose to land on it. This is why Paul writes, "For those whom [God] foreknew he also predestined" (Romans 8:29). But not only that, Jesus goes further to pay for their "rent" so that they come because of Christ's payment and they stay because their dues have been "paid in full." They are, as the Bible states, bought at a price (1 Corinthians 6:20) and their account is fully settled.

God is not in the business of taking risks. He's in the business of purposefully saving his people by grace. He doesn't scatter the breadcrumbs of atonement across the world in hopes that some will happen to see them and eat. No, God sent his Son to die for his people "according to the purpose of his will" (Ephesians 1:5). Christ's death was purposeful, intentional, and definite!

THE TAPESTRY OF GOD

Do you like to draw pictures or paint? You have probably had an art class before in which you learned the "art" of art. When I try to draw a picture on a whiteboard in class or to make an illustration, I oftentimes get laughs. My trees look like clouds and my trumpets look like spaghetti! Art is something I admire, not only because I (usually) find it beautiful, but also because I don't understand it. It's complex and there is something mysterious and deep about the blending of colors to create a masterpiece. The same goes for those who weave together multi-colored garments.

One amazing thing about God is that he is weaving a beautiful tapestry of people "from every nation, from all tribes and peoples and languages" to worship him (Revelation 7:9). This masterpiece, was planned before time began and is being woven as his people come to saving faith in Christ. The Bible tells us that "we are his workmanship, created in Christ Jesus for good works, which God prepared beforehand, that we should walk in them" (Ephesians 2:10). The word for "workmanship" conveys the idea of a beautiful tapestry. You, as a believer in Christ, are part of God's beautiful masterpiece and tapestry!

A painter envisions his painting beforehand, chooses the colors, and then paints those colors in the exact place of his choosing on the canvas. In the same way, God foreknows his people, chooses his people, and saves his people—all of which work together to create a beautiful masterpiece for his glory and his peoples' joy.

In Ephesians 3:10, Paul speaks of the "manifold wisdom of God" in making the church known to the world. What is interesting is that the word for "manifold" is the same word used in the Septuagint (the Greek translation of the Old Testament) for Joseph's coat of "many" colors (Genesis 37:3). In other words, God's wisdom in saving and revealing his church is like a beautiful garment of many colors and patterns, woven together to create one unified tapestry.

The tapestry that God is weaving is not arbitrary, nor does God try a certain type of thread in hopes that it might look good. Nothing could be farther from the truth! God's not a risky weaver. Rather, God sent his only Son to redeem his elect and to usher them into glory. Christ's death on the cross was both sufficient (able to save) and efficient (actually saving).

JESUS GOING "GREEN"

Before my daughter Lydia was born, my wife and I were told it would be a girl. We went shopping (something I typically dread!) and bought girly paint, girly clothes, and girly furniture to match all the girly stuff in her girly bedroom. Then I went to work! I painted her room, assembled the crib and even folded all of Lydia's little pajamas in her chest of drawers. Not only that, we made the house as safe as possible—removing sharp objects and small items that could be picked up and choked on. We were given music that taught the truths of the Bible and we put it in her room. A friend even painted her name on a canvass to hang over her crib. We were preparing the house for Lydia and for no other.

God does the same with us. He planned our redemption in Christ, sent his Son to redeem us, and will bring us into our prepared home in heaven. Jesus said, "In my Father's house are many rooms...If I go and prepare a place *for you*, I will come again and will take you to myself, that where I am you may be also" (John 14:2-3, emphasis added). Jesus didn't ascend into heaven to prepare empty rooms in our heavenly home, but rooms for his people. Jesus preparing a place for his people communicates the idea that we will be with him, which is far greater than any structural mansion. The point is not so much on the architecture of heaven as it is on the consummate union of Christ and his people. Jesus died for those who would abide in his heavenly mansion. Jesus has "gone green"—he doesn't waste any materials for rooms that won't be filled!

OBJECTION: THE "WHOLE WORLD"

The key passage that many who follow "universal atonement" point to is 1 John 2:2, which reads, "[Christ] is the propitiation for our sins, and not for ours only but also for the sins of the whole world." Out of context, this would seem to contradict Reformed theology's understanding of Jesus' purposeful and definite atonement. However, in context, it perfectly dovetails with it.

During the first century A.D., the faith that was once limited to the nation of ancient Israel spread beyond its borders to the "whole world." This was a major shift in thinking to many early Jewish converts to Christianity. For thousands of years, God's people were—for the most part—limited to the Jews. But when Christ came into the world, his own people reject him (John 1:11). The branch of Israel was broken off from the tree of God's people so that the Gentiles (non-Jews) would be grafted into that same tree (Romans 11).

In addition, Jesus tore down "the dividing wall of hostility" between Jew and Gentile (Ephesians 2:14) so that, in him, there is "neither Jew nor Greek," but "all are one in Christ Jesus" (Galatians 3:28). Suddenly all of the Old Testament prophecies that foretold this major event came true. The "nations" foretold from Genesis 12 and throughout the Old Testament would now be included in God's salvation history on a grand scale.

When John writes of Christ's sacrifice of atonement, his Jewish readers would have expected it to be for them because they were God's people to begin with. But, what John is communicating—echoing the other New Testament writers—is that Christ's sacrifice wasn't just for the Jews who would believe in Jesus, but also for people throughout the "whole world!"

Thus, this verse in 1 John doesn't mean that Christ's death atoned for every individual in the whole world, but rather it was purposefully for those who would believe outside of the Jewish household— the Gentiles. This is also why so much of the New Testament is concerned with this major shift in thinking, seen in the debates that take place in the book of Acts and in Paul's writing in the first four chapters of the book of Romans.

A similar point can be made for John 3:16—"For God so loved the world." Yet, other passages state that God "hates" the unbeliever (see Psalm 5:5; Romans 9:13).

How can both of these statements be true? The answer is that God loves his people throughout the whole world. This is a saving and sacrificial love. Moreover, we must be careful when interpreting the word "world."

For example, Paul writes that the Romans' faith "is proclaimed in all the world" (Romans 1:8). Does this mean that the Romans' faith was proclaimed in Antarctica? I don't think so. It is an expression indicating the far-reaching knowledge of the Romans' faith. The point is, we must see these texts in their contexts, historically and from other clearer passages of Scripture.

Christ's atoning work on the cross was purposeful. It was an intentional sacrifice for those for whom he came to die. Just before Jesus' arrest and execution, he prayed to the Father, "I am not praying for the world but for those whom you have given me, for they are yours" (John 17:9).

The Father gave a bride to his Son and his Son purchased that bride with his life. Let us exalt Christ—that he died for us as believers!

 ## REFLECTION QUESTIONS

- Imagine that God takes risks; that he didn't know what would have happened after Jesus' death or who would believe. Is there comfort or hope in this kind of God?

- In your own words explain the idea of Christ's intentional, purposeful, and definite sacrifice of atonement.

- If God elected a people from all eternity past, does it make sense for him to send his Son to die for those who wouldn't believe? Why not?

- How can the doctrine of limited atonement comfort your soul? If you are a believer you are part of God's tapestry. How might that bring comfort to your heart right now?

ONLY THROUGH CHRIST

As a student, you probably meet people from a wide variety of religious backgrounds—Buddhist, Hindu, Mormon, and Islam—to name a few.

Increasingly, the predominant view in the Western world is that all religions are basically the same. They all worship the same God, but express their faith in a variety of different ways. This belief is called "pluralism."

THE ELEPHANT

One of the classic illustrations of pluralism is that of the blind men and the elephant. In this illustration, several blind men (each representing a different religion) are walking and stumble upon an elephant (which represents God). All of the blind men touch a different part of the elephant's body. One touches the elephant's ear, another touches the elephant's leg, and so on. Each of the blind men describes the elephant in different ways, but in the end, it is the same elephant. Each blind man could only feel a part of the elephant, but could not see all of it. This illustration is meant to explain how there are many different religions in the world, but they all ultimately worship the same "God."

However, this illustration has a serious flaw. In a helpful comment in his book, *The Reason for God*, Timothy Keller writes: This illustration backfires on its users. The story is told from someone who is not blind. How could you know that each blind man only sees part of the elephant unless you claim to be able to see the whole elephant?

Keller's point is that the individual who claims that nobody has the whole truth is, by virtue of making that claim, assuming that he or she sees the whole picture. In other words, if someone claims that there is no absolute truth, he or she is—at the same time—making an absolute truth claim. The more you argue against absolute truth, the more you are actually arguing for it!

Believing that faith in Jesus Christ is the only way to be saved is incredibly offensive to more and more people in our day. Why? Because what we are affirming, in effect, is that unless a person surrenders his or her life to the King of kings and Lord of lords—Jesus Christ— he or she will not be saved.

IN CHRIST ALONE

Reformed theology teaches that a person is saved through faith alone in Christ alone. A person, therefore, is not saved from hell and judgment by being a "good" Muslim, Buddhist, or Mormon. Paul writes of his lost Jewish brethren, "For I bear them witness that they have a zeal for God, but not according to knowledge" (Romans 10:2). Having a "zeal" for any god other than the triune God of the Bible only turns in the wages of sin, which is death (Romans 6:23).

Luke writes in the book of Acts, "And there is salvation in no one else, for there is no other name under heaven given among men by which we must be saved" (Acts 4:12). It could hardly be stated any clearer: There is salvation in no one but Jesus Christ. This statement might make your friends at school and possibly your parents become angry. It's not popular. But then, Jesus wasn't popular either. Jesus was the only righteous One who ever walked this earth and sinners nailed him to a cross.

THE WAY, THE TRUTH, AND THE LIFE

Do you ask a lot of questions? Would others consider you a curious person? Sometimes curiosity can get us into trouble. For "doubting" Thomas, it brought on one of the most powerful statements from Jesus' lips in the New Testament. Thomas asked him, "Lord, how can we know the way?" speaking about the way of salvation. Jesus answered: "I am the way, and the truth, and the life. No one comes to the Father except through me" (John 14:6). Look at the different parts to Jesus' answer. First, he says that he is the way, which means that there is not another way to be saved. Elsewhere, Jesus says, "I am the door. If anyone enters by me, he will be saved" (John 10:9). The only way by which we are saved is through Christ.

Second, Jesus says that he is the truth. We've already noted the importance of truth above, but Jesus clearly indicates that there is truth. In fact, he is the truth. If you feel bombarded by a constant barrage of lies and half-truths, look unto Christ, the Rock unchanging, who is called "Faithful and True" (Revelation 19:11). He is true and his words are pure (Psalm 12:6).

Third, Jesus says that he is the life. The Author of life is also the "author and perfecter of our faith" (Hebrews 12:2). All who put their faith in Jesus and him alone will "not perish but have eternal life" (John 3:16). Salvation is offered only through the "bread of life" (John 6:35) so that "by believing you may have life in his name" (John 20:31). Other breads mold.

But look at the second part of Jesus' statement again: "No one comes to the Father except through me." Imagine that Jesus only said, "No one comes to the Father." If God wanted this to be the message, he would have been perfectly just to do so. But, God offers one exception— faith in Jesus Christ! No one can come to God the Father except through Jesus. No matter how many people tell you that all religions are basically the same or that they all worship the same God, Jesus remains crystal clear: there is salvation in no one else.

THE CONTENT OF FAITH

But what do we mean that salvation is in Christ alone? Reformed theology points to the fact that the content of the message of salvation is the gospel. The gospel includes several parts. First, the gospel means "good news," which necessarily assumes that there is "bad news." The bad news (as we have seen) is that all mankind is fallen and, apart from God's work of grace, under his just judgment and condemnation. You and I are more sinful than we could ever imagine. We don't often even understand the evil intentions of our hearts!

Second, the content of the gospel is that believers are declared "not guilty" and "righteous" before God because Jesus died the death you should have died and lived the life you should have lived—fulfilling all of God's commandments—on your behalf. This is known as the doctrine of justification. Notice that the believer is not made righteous (that will take place in heaven), but declared righteous. Righteousness is the reward of perfect obedience. Christ was perfectly obedient to all of God's commandments. By faith, your sin is laid upon Jesus and his righteousness is laid upon you. Upon this "great exchange," you are declared righteous in God's sight, as if you have fulfilled and perfectly obeyed all of God's commandments. That is the core of the gospel. That is the good news that we proclaim. That is the content of salvation "in Christ alone."

Third, this gospel is received by faith alone. It is important to point out that salvation is not in Christ plus something else. That would mean that salvation is not in Christ alone. Rather, Reformed theology teaches that faith is the hand that clings to Christ, while recognizing that even faith is a gift. The Scriptures say, "For by grace you have been saved through faith. And this is not your own doing; it is the gift of God, not as a result of works, so that no one may boast" (Ephesians 2:8-9). Reformed theology emphasizes that a person is not justified before God by works, but by faith alone (cf. Galatians 2:15-21).

IS JESUS SERIOUS?

When I was fifteen years old, I was taking a course in astronomy in school. The teacher handed out a syllabus, which outlined the requirements for the class—two exams and one long paper on the planet Saturn. I remember one of my friends asking the teacher, "Can I pick a different topic to write about, something other than Saturn?" The teacher's answer: "Absolutely not! You write what I assign." It was clear; there was no getting around the assigned paper or the topic. And we all did it. No one even thought about doing a paper on a different topic after that.

But, let's say that one of my friends did a paper on, say, Pluto. If he had tried to hand it to the teacher, my teacher would have simply rejected it. Even if the student wrote a paper twice as long and included more sources than necessary (and who would do that!), he still would have failed because he didn't follow the guidelines explained by the teacher.

Similarly, many people simply disregard what Jesus said. Their attitude goes something like "Yeah, I know Jesus said that he's the only way and all, but he isn't really serious, is he?" I'm afraid that many people who are cruising through life thinking that, in the end, Jesus will accept them on their terms will be greatly mistaken. He will say to them on that day, "I never knew you; depart from me you workers of lawlessness" (Matthew 7:23).

The biblical writers are absolutely clear that there is salvation in no one else but Christ. He is the only door through which men and women, boys and girls may be saved. While secularism, pluralism and other religions compete for your allegiance in this life, Christ remains the only Savior of sinners. He is the Judge of the living and the dead (2 Timothy 4:1) and there will come a day when every knee will bow and "confess that Jesus Christ is Lord, to the glory of God the Father" (Philippians 2:10-11).

 ## REFLECTION QUESTIONS

- As you consider the biblical truth that salvation is only through Jesus Christ, do you personally know somebody that might take offence at this? What is their main objection?

- If there was no absolute truth in the universe, do you think there could be true "right" or "wrong"? Why or why not?

- Can you think of any other passages in the Bible that speaks about Jesus being the only Savior?

- If there was another Savior, what would that do to the credibility of Jesus' teaching and message?

- Knowing that salvation is only through Jesus, what should your response be to an unbelieving world? To your friends? To your family?

RESTING BY FAITH ALONE

Do you have a "best" friend? If you had to pick someone, who would it be? My best friend growing up was Aaron and Aaron was good at everything! He was smart, good-looking and athletic. He played varsity soccer and even graduated from high school first in his class. I, on the other hand, was not very smart, good looking or athletic—which oftentimes made me a little jealous of Aaron's seemingly effortless perfection.

I had a difficult time doing my schoolwork. I just wasn't interested. "What does Henry VIII have to do with me?" I would often think to myself. Despite my difficulties, I knew that if I was to do well in a course, I had to earn it! The teacher was not going to just give me a grade that I didn't deserve. Aaron understood this. Aaron earned perfect grades; I didn't. He applied himself; I didn't. He even received money from his parents for doing well; I didn't (though that might have given me some incentive!).

However, I praise God that salvation is not like this. In God's school, he chooses his students, saves them by grace alone through faith alone and equips them to do the work he has assigned. God's students don't earn his favor, grace or salvation. He grants it freely, and they receive it by faith alone.

The amazing thing about the gospel is that your final exam has already been aced for you by another—Jesus Christ. Christ has not only suffered the consequences of our failure, but has also earned a perfect score for all who believe in him as Savior and Lord. In fact, Scripture tells us that Jesus became sin (our failures) so that we might become the righteousness of God (his perfection) (cf. 2 Corinthians 5:21). On the basis of this great exchange, God looks at our exam and declares it, "Perfect!"

SOLA FIDE

One of the battle cries—if not the main battle cry—of the Protestant Reformation in the sixteenth century was the Latin phrase *sola fide*—"by faith alone." But what did the Reformers mean by this phrase? They meant that a person is accepted and saved by God by believing in Jesus Christ. Or, to put it another way, they argued that no amount of good works could save a sinner.

All of the Bible-reading, prayer-offering and church-going that you could do in your lifetime could not earn you any favor with God. Rather, sinners are saved by faith alone in Christ alone and loved unconditionally (cf. Romans 8:37-39)! The Bible states that 'all who rely on works of the law are under a curse" (Galatians 3:10). If you are currently relying on your good works to save you, make no mistake: you are still under God's curse.

During the sixteenth century, Protestants (as they became known) "protested" against the abuses and theology of the Roman Catholic Church. Catholic theology teaches that salvation comes as a result of faith plus works, not faith alone. But what the Reformers saw in Scripture is that sinners cannot build up their pile of works in hope that their good deeds will weigh the heavenly balance in their favor. Rather, God has entered into this fallen world as a man, to redeem a people for himself, and that those people would receive this unmerited gift of God by simply believing.

But it is important to emphasize that even this believing is a gift from God. The Bible states, "For by grace you have been saved through faith. And this is not your own doing; it is the gift of God, not a result of works, so that no one may boast" (Ephesians 2:8-9). Faith—indeed, the entire work of salvation—is the gift of God. Why? So that you and I cannot boast about our accomplishments before him and therefore steal the glory that is due only to God alone. It is God who has saved us. It is God who has given us faith. And it is God who will bring us into our heavenly home.

JUSTIFICATION

Central to this belief of *sola fide* is the doctrine of justification. Justification is the judicial act whereby God declares a sinner "not guilty". This declaration is pronounced upon a person when he or she receives the gift of salvation by faith alone, not by doing good works.

The apostle Paul writes, "We know that a person is not justified by works of the law but through faith in Jesus Christ" (Galatians 2:16). With equal clarity, he explains elsewhere, "For we hold that one is justified by faith apart from works of the law" (Romans 3:28). Justification, then, is a gracious and free act of God whereby he declares us "just" in his sight through faith in his Son, Jesus Christ.

Imagine a courtroom scene. The accused murderer stands to hear his verdict read by the judge. The evidence is overwhelming in favor of his guilt. Voice recording has captured his murderous intentions. Video surveillance has captured the murderous act. There is no question that he is guilty as charged.

Then the judge reads the verdict: "The accused is found not guilty!" How could that be? How could the accused be justified when he is clearly guilty? In terms of salvation, the only way that sinners may be justified is by faith alone in the finished work of Christ alone.

But what is the work of Christ and the basis on which God declares sinners righteous in his sight? The basis is two fold.

First, the punishment and condemnation that we deserve has been fully placed on Christ. That is why he had to die on a cross. Second, Christ's righteousness—the reward of his perfect obedience to all of God's commands—is transferred to us. On that basis, God declares us "not guilty"!

In the book of Revelation, Jesus says that he will give the believer a "white stone, with a new name written on the stone" (Revelation 2:17). In ancient times, members of a jury would cast their vote with either a black stone—representing a guilty verdict—or a white stone—representing an innocent verdict. Jesus, as it were, has cast his vote with a white stone, declaring all true believers "innocent." The reason is that he himself has become our sin as the sacrificial Lamb of God and his innocence has been credited to our account.

CHRIST'S WORK FOR YOU

I used to work in a lumberyard, stacking boards made of oak, pine, spruce and maple. I also had to band the stacks together and load lumber onto customers' trucks. I remember the early summer mornings, when the air was cool and the flowers where in full bloom. It felt good to work and to earn a little income. My uncle, who owned the lumberyard, would give me a checklist every day of tasks that needed to be completed. It was my job to work through that checklist, making sure I didn't miss anything.

I was fourteen years old at the time and surprised when, one day, my uncle gave me the keys to drive a three-ton forklift! I had no idea what I was doing, but driving this piece of machinery made my day. There is something about driving a big machine that gives a young man a sense of power. However, because I was inexperienced with driving it, I routinely knocked over neatly stacked piles of lumber and even managed to put a hole through the fence surrounding the property. Customers became increasingly unhappy, and so did my uncle!

That summer, I learned the difference between working to earn my uncle's trust and acceptance as an employee and working in such a way as to lose his trust and acceptance. The determining factor was the quality of my work.

In a similar way, Jesus' work was of perfect quality. What was Jesus' work? He prayed just before his arrest and subsequent execution, "I glorified you on earth, having accomplished the work that you gave me to do" (John 17:4). While Christ's "work" certainly included his sacrifice of atonement on the cross, it also included his life of perfect obedience to his Father in heaven.

It should be emphasized that Jesus was tempted with sin in every way—just like you and me (Hebrews 4:15). Yet, he never gave in. He never sinned. Even when facing the gruesome and excruciating pain of the cross, he prayed, "Not my will, but yours, be done" (Luke 22:42). Because he never gave in to temptation, he knew the full weight of it. You and I easily succumb to the temptation of sin. As soon as it knocks, we open the door to it. But Christ never opened the door to sin. The temptation just kept knocking.

Jesus resisted temptation so that he would live a sinless life—on your behalf. When God looks upon you, as a believer, he doesn't see you still in your sin and misery. He sees you clothed in the righteousness and sinlessness of his Son. Because of that, he takes great delight in calling you his adopted child, with all of the privileges and rights of being a son or daughter of God.

RIGHTEOUSNESS BY FAITH

Reformed theology teaches that a person receives the righteousness of Christ by faith alone, not works. In communicating this idea from the story of Abraham in Genesis, the apostle Paul writes, "Abraham believed God, and it was counted to him as righteousness" (Romans 4:3). By simply believing, Abraham was counted as righteous in God's sight. Paul writes elsewhere that he is found in Christ not by "having a righteousness of my own that comes from the law, but that which comes through faith in Christ, the righteousness from God that depends on faith" (Philippians 3:9).

Righteousness is the reward for perfect obedience. Since you and I are not perfect, we must receive it from Someone who was. This is why the Bible states that it is righteousness from God that depends on faith. Righteousness is earned, like the wages of my work in the lumberyard. However, our works—as "good" as we might like them to be—are like filthy rags. Isaiah explains, "We have all become like one who is unclean, and all our righteous deeds are like a polluted garment" (Isaiah 64:6). Because our works are clothed in sin, our wages are death and hell forever (Romans 6:23).

But because Jesus' works were pure and sinless, his wage is righteousness. All that you need to do in order to be accepted by a holy and just God has already been done for you. Jesus has worked for you so that you—having already been eternally accepted by God—may work for him!

ARE WE FREE TO SIN?

This raises an obvious question: If Jesus is your righteousness by faith alone, and you can do nothing to change your status as an adopted child of God, then why not go and sin? In other words, sinning would make God be more gracious, right?

Paul asks it like this, "Are we to continue in sin that grace may abound?" Answer: "By no means!" (Romans 6:1-2). While we are saved by faith alone, faith is never alone. Faith is always evidenced by good works or the "fruit of the spirit—love, joy, peace, patience, kindness, goodness, faithfulness, gentleness and self-control" (Galatians 5:22-23). James writes that "faith by itself, if it does not have works, is dead" (James 2:17). If you are truly a believer in Christ, then you will want to please God with your life. The fruit of good works is the evidence of a living tree of faith.

St. Augustine (A.D. 354-430) once made the comment, "Love God and do whatever you want." His point was that if your desire is for God, then you will naturally want to do that which pleases him. While it is by faith alone that we receive the gift of salvation, faith always produces good works.

 ### REFLECTION QUESTIONS

- If God's love depended upon how good you were—how much you went to church or how much you prayed—then what would that say about the nature of God's love? Would it be conditional or unconditional love? Why?

- Why is it important that salvation is received by faith alone and not works? Why might it be important that salvation isn't received by faith plus works?

- If you were saved by good works, is there any real need for Jesus?

- What is the "basis" of justification, of God declaring you not guilty? What are the two parts of this declaration?

MASTERED BY GRACE

I love backpacking. There's nothing like hiking into a remote destination (especially in the mountains), pitching a tent and enjoying a dinner cooked over an open fire. Even potted meat tastes amazing in the middle of the woods!

If you have ever been camping like this, you know that rain can be a real downer. On one particular trip, several of my friends and I were backpacking in the Appalachian Mountains located along the eastern side of the United States. We were only about two miles in on a ten-mile trip when the skies opened up and it started pouring! Even though the rain only lasted about twenty minutes, I was soaked—especially my boots.

After the rains stopped, my friends stopped and put on dry socks from their backpacks. I didn't. I just wanted to get to the campsite, even though it was still eight miles ahead. I paid for that decision. After about an hour, my feet were burning and I was developing some big blisters. But, I pressed on. I even resisted my friends' offer to stop, playing it off as if it wasn't that bad. I was trying to be a true man who doesn't feel pain!

When we arrived at the campsite that evening, I had blisters all over my feet. Some were bleeding. Because of my pride, my feet were badly hurt and we had to change our hiking schedule for that trip.

GRANTED TO COME

Like my pride in resisting the rest and comfort of my friends' offer to stop, God is resisted until God chooses to overcome the sinner by grace. Those who remain in their sin remain in their stubbornness and resistance. They remain rebels at heart! The reason for this is that the unbeliever—apart from God's overcoming grace—is completely unable to come to God on his or her own (Romans 8:7).

Reformed theology teaches that, when God effectually draws a person to faith in Christ, that person will surely come. Historically, this is called the doctrine of Irresistible Grace. Before time began God chose a people to be saved. Jesus taught, "All that the Father gives me will come to me, and whoever comes to me I will never cast out" (John 6:37). The Father gives his people to his Son and those people "will come" to him.

Jesus said, "No one can come to me unless the Father who sent me draws him" (John 6:44). The word for "draw" here means more than simple enticing and wooing. For example, in Acts 16:19, Paul and Silas are "dragged" into prison. The same Greek word is used. If the Father "draws" a sinner by grace to Christ, he will surely come by grace to Christ. In the same chapter where Paul and Silas are dragged into prison, a woman named Lydia hears the gospel preached by Paul. Luke writes, "The Lord opened her heart to pay attention to what was said by Paul" (Acts 16:14).

Jesus clarifies this point even further: "No one can come to me unless it is granted him by the Father" (John 6:65). Note Jesus' use of the word "unless." The only way that we can enter into a saving relationship with Jesus is if God the Father "grants" us to come. Apart from this gracious act of God, no one can come to Jesus.

THE SECOND BIRTH

Typically, nothing good happens late at night. That's when thieves break in and steal. That's when evil plots are executed. Under the cover of darkness, all sorts of bad things happen. But, there's always the exception.

One of these exceptions came when a Pharisee and ruler of the Jews named Nicodemus "came to Jesus by night" (John 3:2). He had some questions that he probably felt embarrassed to ask in broad daylight. He didn't want to ruin his reputation in the Jewish community. So this "Nick at Night" shows up during the time of Passover in Jerusalem.

Nicodemus tells Jesus, "Rabbi, we know that you are a teacher come from God, for no one can do these signs that you do" (v. 2). Jesus said to him, "Truly, truly, I say to you, unless one is born again he cannot see the kingdom of God" (v. 3). At this, Nicodemus was confused and didn't understand. He asks, "How can a man be born when he is old? Can he enter a second time into his mother's womb and be born?" (v. 4).

If we were there, we might ask the same thing. How can a person be born again? Jesus' answer is remarkable: "Truly, truly, I say to you, unless one is born of water and the Spirit, he cannot enter the kingdom of God. That which is born of the flesh is flesh, and that which is born of the Spirit is spirit" (v. 5-6). Everyone is born into this world somehow. I'll let you do the research on that! But only those who are "born of the Spirit" can enter the kingdom of God. This second birth—called regeneration—is something that God does.

GOD'S GRACIOUS WILL

You have probably seen a variety of styles of music in churches around where you live. Sometimes, this variety has led to "worship wars" within the church. The battles lines are often drawn between traditional and contemporary, reverent and celebratory. However, biblically-based, gospel-driven, Christ-centered and Reformed songs and hymns are being written all the time. In a recent hymn—"Hymn to a Gracious Sovereign" (2005)—Neil Barham penned these words:

O God the deep immutable,
the changeless, wise and still,
You're the absolute, eternal One;
You wield the sovereign will.
Deep Heav'n itself and even time
must bend beneath your sway.
With a whispered thought you banish
night in a flash of blinding day.

What's interesting about this hymn is the stress upon God's sovereignty. Typically, God's sovereignty is brushed under the rug because it is oftentimes offensive. However, there is an important lesson to learn here.

If a person could resist God's sovereign will, God's will would cease to be sovereign. We've learned already that all things, including our salvation, happen "according to the purpose of [God's] will" (Ephesians 1:5). God's will is that which he desires to do and then put into action. It is desire made effective. Or, to put it another way, it is God's desire and purpose displayed in time and space.

In Romans 9:19, the apostle Paul asks the rhetorical question, "Who can resist his will?" Answer: Nobody. We don't even have the right to raise any objection to

God's sovereign will. God is God and is perfectly free to do that which he pleases. For God's elect, God graciously performs a divine heart transplant, replacing your "heart of stone" (Ezekiel 36:26) with one that loves and desires him. If God calls you by grace, you will surely come by grace.

I'VE CALLED YOU BY NAME!

One of my favorite books is *The Pilgrim's Progress* by John Bunyan. It is one of the best-selling books of all time. It tells the story of Christian and his journey from the City of Destruction to the Celestial City of heaven. Along the way, he encounters all sorts of dangers and violent people. He also meets a few friends. One of these friends is Hopeful.

In a dramatic scene, Christian and Hopeful find themselves crossing a great River (symbolizing death). Christian sees the waves rising up and he begins to doubt whether or not he can make it to the Celestial City. But he remembers God's promise from Isaiah: "Fear not, for I have redeemed you; I have called you by name, you are mine. When you pass through the waters, I will be with you; and through the rivers, they shall not overwhelm you" (Isaiah 43:1-2).

Bunyan then writes, "Christian therefore presently found ground to stand upon, and so it followed that the rest of the river was but shallow; but thus they got over." God calls his people by name. His calling is the solid ground when all other callings in this world are but sinking sand.

If you are called to Jesus by grace, you are justified. If you are justified, then you will be glorified. As Paul writes, "And those whom he predestined he also called, and those whom he called he also justified, and those whom he justified he also glorified" (Romans 8:30). The apostle Peter links God's calling and eternal election together when he writes, "Be all the more diligent to confirm your calling and election" (2 Peter 1:10).

By grace, God calls sinners to come to Jesus. He removes the wet socks and stony hearts and clothes us with Christ, in whom we find eternal rest (cf. Matthew 11:28). He stops me on the trail of life to give me a new life in Jesus. "He makes me lie down in green pastures. He leads me beside still waters.

He restores my soul" (Psalm 23:1-3). May you delight this day in the God who draws you to himself so that the grace that brought you safe thus far, is the grace that will lead you home.

REFLECTION QUESTIONS

- How might the idea that, if God "calls" you by grace, you will surely come to saving faith bring you comfort?

- Were any parts of this chapter difficult to either believe or understand?

- Could the doctrine of God's sovereign election fit with a belief that denies God's actual and providential saving of a person in space and time?

- What are some ways in which you could specifically praise God for his irresistible grace?

ENJOYING GOD'S WORD

I am very glad that books are no longer hand-written. If this book were not in the nice font that you see, it would look like something that resembled chicken scratch—my handwriting is that bad! You wouldn't make it very far.

Before about 1450—when Gutenberg invented the printing press—everything was written by hand. Nothing was mass-produced and, therefore, relatively few people read or could read. In addition, Roman Catholic priests gave their homilies in Latin, which most people didn't even understand.

But the printing press could mass-produce a pamphlet or book and it could quickly be distributed all over Europe— and beyond! Soon, everybody wanted to read and a new wave of learning burst onto the European scene.

By 1517, when Martin Luther nailed his 95 Theses to the church door in Wittenberg, Germany, the printing press was a well-oiled machine. Reformed theology could be quickly printed and distributed and could rally large masses of people for a common goal with great speed. Luther's declarations against the Roman Catholic Church were immediately published and sent all over Germany and the Reformation began!

WHO'S THE BOSS?

One of the fundamental changes that came with the Protestant Reformation was recognition of a new authority—the Bible. While the Bible certainly held a central place in the Roman Catholic Church, it shared its authority with the Pope and Church Tradition. This triplet—Bible, Pope, and Tradition—were held together as a woven cord of sacred authority.

The Reformers taught, however, that the church's authority should rest, not upon any man or tradition, but upon Scripture alone—a doctrine known as *Sola Scriptura.* God's Word, they argued, is sufficient for both faith and the practice of the church. The Bible was to have supreme authority over all men and all tradition.

As a man cannot serve two masters, so also Christians cannot serve two supreme authorities. Indeed, the very idea of "supreme" conveys oneness. Reformed theology places that supreme authority for the church in the Word of God because it is God's self-revelation.

HERE COMES THE SUN!

I'm not a morning guy. My wife, on the other hand, can wake up early and be full of life! I take a little while to get going. Maybe you can relate. You might have to wake up early for school or for athletic practice. But most teenagers are like me— they love their sleep!

For many Christians around the world, a portion of the morning is set-aside for an individual devotional time in the Word. Whether it's an actual Bible study or a reflective reading of Scripture, Christians around the world believe that time in God's Word and prayer is the best way to start the day.

This practice, however, was made popular during the Reformation and the generations that immediately followed. While believers have practiced Scripture meditation from the earliest days of the church, it was not until the Reformation and Post-Reformation that the practice of personal Bible study became a regular practice in many households.

Because Scripture is our sole authority for faith and life, Reformed theology sees the beauty of personal Bible study. It sees the beauty of family Bible study. It sees the beauty of Bible study at church, at school and with friends. Reading God's Word, however, isn't to be a legalistic law, but an enjoyable delight.

BREATHED-OUT BY GOD

I've mentioned that I enjoy backpacking. But I cannot stand backpacking or camping in the summertime. There is no escaping the heat and bugs. Moreover, making a fire in the middle of the summer only makes the situation that much more uncomfortable.

But camping in the wintertime is wonderful! The fire feels so warm and, if there's snow on the ground, you have the added bonus of having plenty of available water—not to mention an occasional snowball fight with friends!

On one particular camping trip, it was so cold that my breath actually froze to the inside of my tent. Every time I bumped the side of the tent, a light dusting of snow blanketed my sleeping bag and clothes. I found it fascinating that my breath, which I could not see in the tent, became something solid.

Similarly, God's Word was "breathed out by God" (2 Timothy 3:16). It is from him and written down by human writers. These biblical writers were "carried along by the Holy Spirit" (2 Peter 1:21) as they wrote so that it truly is the Word of God to man. The Bible is inspired by God. It has God as its ultimate author, while—at the same time—it was written by the hand of man.

THE ONE AND ONLY

Of all the books ever written in the history of the world, only one bears the superlative of being divine revelation. The Bible is utterly unique. Not only is it unique in being the best selling and most-read book of all time, it is unique in the fact that it alone has God as the author.

There are two basic kinds of revelation. First, God has revealed himself in creation. The Psalmist declares, "The heavens declare the glory of God, and the sky above proclaims his handiwork" (Psalm 19:1). Creation is God's general revelation. The Bible, on the other hand, is God's special revelation. While God has revealed enough about himself in his creation to make all humanity knowledgeable of his power and nature (Romans 1:19-20), he has accommodated himself to our frail and limited understanding by revealing his eternal plan of salvation in his Word.

No other book in the history of the world has been so studied, so scrutinized and so examined as the Bible. Even still, it has stood the test of time. It remains the one and only divinely inspired book. All sixty-six books that make up the Bible point to the manifold perfection of God and his glorious grace in the gospel of Jesus Christ (cf. Luke 24:27, 44).

Moreover, because the revelation given for Scripture has ceased with the close of the apostolic age (cf. 1 Corinthians 13:8; Revelation 22:18), what we have is sufficient and efficient to make us wise for salvation.

FROM CHILDHOOD, ACQUAINTED

The apostle Paul writes to Timothy, "From childhood you have been acquainted with the sacred writings, which are able to make you wise for salvation through faith in Christ Jesus" (2 Timothy 3:15). Timothy grew up learning about God in his Word. His grandmother Lois and mother Eunice taught him the truths of Scripture (2 Timothy 1:5).

Did you learn about the Bible growing up? Maybe you've never read it before? If you haven't, there is no better time to start than now! God's Word is "a lamp to my feet and a light to my path" (Psalm 119:105). Storing up God's Word in our hearts helps us fight sin, addiction and destructive habits (cf. Psalm 119:11).

Have you ever been in a room full of people, but yet felt lonely? It's possible and actually happens quite often. You can be around people without knowing them. The same is true with Scripture. Many self-proclaiming Christians today are "around" Scripture—they hear about it or they see it on a bookshelf. But many do not know it. They are not "acquainted" with it. Why is that? There are several probable reasons.

The Bible can be a difficult read, especially without a study guide or commentary. There are some who pick up the Bible intending to read it in its entirety, but make it into the bloody sections of the Levitical law (the third book in the Bible) or the lists of the book of Numbers (the fourth book) and confusion has them put it down. Then, they forever say, "I gave it a shot" or "I tried it, but found it lacking."

Perhaps you have tried reading the Bible and found it daunting. I would suggest getting plugged into a Bible-believing church where it is regularly preached and taught. I would also suggest picking up a study guide, a commentary or even a study Bible (one that includes notations) to help you. May the Bible be a source of living water to your soul!

THE SWORD OF THE SPIRIT

Before we conclude this chapter, there is one more important element in understanding the importance of this Reformed belief in Scripture. In Ephesians, chapter six, Paul writes about the "armor of God." The pieces of armor include: the belt of truth, the breastplate of righteousness, the shoes of the gospel of peace, the shield of faith, the helmet of salvation, and the sword of the Spirit.

Interestingly, this last one—the "sword of the Spirit"—is called "the Word of God" (Ephesians 6:17). How is God's Word like a sword? The writer of Hebrews points out, "The word of God is living and active, sharper than any two-edged sword, piercing to the division of soul and spirit, of joints and of marrow, and discerning the thoughts and intentions of the heart" (Hebrews 4:12). Similarly, the apostle John writes that out of Jesus' mouth shall come a symbolic "two-edged sword" with which he will judge (Revelation 1:16).

These references show us that God's Word acts like a sword to both defend believers and attack the enemy. Hiding God's Word in your heart brings great defense when you find yourself under spiritual attack or under the pressures of this world. It reminds us of our true identity and security in Christ, no matter what happens in this life.

But God's Word is also an offensive weapon against the forces of this evil world, Satan and sin. Interestingly, the word used in Ephesians, chapter six for "word" is the more-unusual *rhema* in Greek, which refers to the spoken word as opposed to the written word (*logos*). Knowing the word, we are able to speak it. God's Word, then, becomes an offensive weapon when, having hidden his Word in your heart, you know it and use it.

In *The Pilgrim's Progress,* Christian finds himself fighting the evil dragon Apollyon. Almost defeated, Christian pulls out the "sword of the Spirit" and begins to speak Scripture at the dragon. Immediately, the dragon leaves. In the same way, God's Word serves to repel the attacks of the world, the flesh and Satan.

Reformed theology teaches that the Word of God is our sole authority for faith and living. It is unique in having God as its ultimate author, even though he "carried along" various human writers. The Bible is breathed-out by God and is therefore of great profit for his people. May you take up and read his Word as a duty of delight!

REFLECTION QUESTIONS

- Do you have regular time in God's Word? If not, what changes can you make in your daily routine?

- What are some common objections to memorizing Scripture? Do those objections have any substance to them?

- How might knowing God's Word be helpful in times of suffering?

- Read 2 Corinthians 2:5-11 several times. What verse stands out to you? Read it several times. What single word stands out? Meditate upon that word and the context around it and ask the Lord to apply that truth to your heart and mind today.

DESIGNED FOR GLORY

I have a big yellow flashlight in my bedroom. I typically do not use it unless I am searching for something outside or playing "flashlight tag." If I need to locate something in my house or in the basement, I'll use a smaller, less-intense flashlight. But my yellow flashlight is big, bright and can shine a spot of light down the entire street that I live on.

The purpose of that flashlight is to shine light. That's what it was made for. That's what it was designed for. You might be able to find other uses for it. I'm sure it would do great at killing a spider or even a small mouse. But that's not its design. The light is the expression and display of the flashlight's design.

In the same way, God's glory is the expression and display of his divine and perfect character. All that has been created, ordained and brought forth in time and space is meant to simply reflect back to God the radiance and brilliance of his own character. As the Psalmist exclaims, "The heavens declare the glory of God, and the sky above proclaims his handiwork" (Psalm 19:1).

When we "glorify" God, we exalt his perfect character and attributes. The clearest expression of his perfect character and attributes is seen in God taking on human flesh in Jesus Christ. Paul writes, 'For God, who said, "Let light shine out of darkness," has shone in our hearts to give the light of the knowledge of the glory of God in the face of Jesus Christ" (2 Corinthians 4:6).

God's glory, like that flashlight, was ultimately displayed when "a child is born and a son is given" (Isaiah 9:6). In Christ, all of the fullness of the glory of God was pleased to dwell (cf. Colossians 1:19; 2:9). Jesus is the image of the invisible God (Colossians 1:15 and deserving of all glory and honor.

GOD ON DISPLAY

The word 'glory' is typically used in three different ways. First, it is used to describe the sum total and expression of God's manifold perfections and attributes. Second, it is used to describe the praise and honor that Christians give to God. Third, it is used to describe the believer's translation into heaven—the "glorified" state.

One of the amazing things about God's glory is that it is inexorably linked to his divine attributes. Glory, in this first sense, is God's character and attributes on display.

I remember walking around the streets of London in 2002 while studying abroad. Street after street of clothing stores, shops, used bookstores and various restaurants provided endless wandering, looking and browsing. If the store has a big front window, it will usually display its best merchandise for sale—outfits, luggage, designer jeans or the latest fiction novel.

In this first sense, God's glory displays all that God is and has to offer. It is the sum total of his manifold perfections expressed throughout the universe. The purpose? That he might be glorified.

THE CHIEF END OF YOU

As an expression of Reformed theology, the Westminster Confession of Faith and the Larger and Shorter Catechisms were written in the 1640s at Westminster Abbey in London. They provide an organized summary of biblical theology.

The first question of the Westminster Shorter Catechism—"What is the chief end of man?"—is answered: "Man's chief end is to glorify God and to enjoy him forever." Your purpose in life, your design, is to exalt God and to magnify his perfect character, which is expressed throughout the universe, his Word, and his Son. But note the second part: to enjoy God.

John Piper, in *Desiring God*, explains that the greatest way that we can glorify God is by enjoying him. Putting it, then, back into the structure of the Catechism, Piper writes, "The chief end of man is to glorify God by enjoying him forever." While glory is God's character expressed, we glorify God when we reflect back to him that perfect character. The way in which we principally do this is by counting him as the greatest Treasure in the universe. The reason that our chief end is to glorify

God and to enjoy him forever is because that is also the chief end of God: to glorify himself and to enjoy himself forever.

Reformed theology teaches that we are to glorify God in all that we do, not just in the worship service on Sundays. In your schoolwork, in your sports and even in your eating and drinking, we are to worship God. Paul writes, "So, whether you eat or drink, or whatever you do, do all to the glory of God" (1 Corinthians 10:31).

The Bible repeatedly calls us to give God glory. We must be careful, however, to note that we are actually not giving God something that he doesn't already have. Rather, when we say that we "give" God glory, we are simply expressing the fact that we are reflecting back to him what he has already expressed to us.

For example, King David wrote, "Ascribe to the LORD, O heavenly beings, ascribe to the LORD glory and strength. Ascribe to the LORD the glory due his name; worship the LORD in the splendor of holiness" (Psalm 29:1-2). Isaiah calls the people to "give glory to the LORD, and declare his praise" (Isaiah 42:12). Giving glory to God, then, is worshipping him for his character, worth and attributes.

SOLI DEO GLORIA

One of the battle cries of the Reformation was *Soli Deo Gloria*—to God alone be the glory! Because it is God who has predestined us, called us, justified us, and sanctifies us, he deserves all of the honor and praise. All the glory is due to him, not man.

After detailing the theology of the gospel and the engrafting of Gentiles into the covenant promises of God in the first eleven chapters of Romans, Paul breaks out with overwhelming praise of God:

"Oh, the depth of the riches and wisdom and knowledge of God! How unsearchable are his judgments and how inscrutable his ways! 'For who has known the mind of the Lord, or who has been his counselor? Or who has given a gift to him that he might be repaid?' For from him and through him and to him are all things. To him be glory forever. Amen" (Romans 11:33-36).

All things, all events, all people, all "catastrophes", all schoolwork, all lakes, all mountains, all money, all empires and nations are meant to bring God glory. It is all designed to magnify his perfect character.

PERSEVERANCE OF THE SAINTS

If the word "glory" is used to describe the display of God's character and our worship of that perfect character, it is also used to describe our transition from this earthly journey into our heavenly home.

Historically speaking, the truth that the believer will be brought home to glory by God's grace, is called the *perseverance of the saints.* Some prefer to use the word "preservation" because it is God who preserves his elect to the end. But they're two sides of the same coin: those who persevere to the end are preserved by God, and those who are preserved by God persevere to the end. As the apostle Paul writes, "He who began a good work in you will bring it to completion at the day of Jesus Christ" (Philippians 1:6). Jesus taught, "I give them eternal life, and they will never perish, and no one will snatch them out of my hand" (John 10:28). What wonderful news! If you're truly a child of God—through faith alone in Christ alone—then you are held by a love that will not let you go.

I don't know if you have ever been a member of a club or an organization before, but typically being a member carries with it certain privileges *and* responsibilities. There are both rewards and duties. If you are a Christian, you are also a *citizen* of heaven. That is your true home and reward. We are but pilgrims passing through this troubled world and have the duty of pursuing Christ even as we have the delight of being transformed into his image.

When Jesus returns, he "will transform our lowly body to be like his glorious body" (Philippians 3:21). Even now, "we all, with unveiled face, beholding the glory of the Lord, are being transformed into the same image from one degree of glory to another" (2 Corinthians 3:18). What this means is that God is making us more and more into the image of his Son, Jesus Christ.

We were created in the image of God (Genesis 1:27). Even though the image and relationship with God was shattered by the Fall (cf. Genesis 3), it is being renewed by the power of God through faith in Christ. Therefore, we are being transformed daily and will be transformed ultimately when Christ returns.

The glory of God will be central to our heavenly worship. With the saints throughout the ages and "from every nation, from all tribes and peoples and languages," we will stand before the throne and before the Lamb and worship! We will join with the heavenly throng of angels and heavenly beings, saying, "Blessing and glory and wisdom and thanksgiving and honor and power and might be to our God forever and ever! Amen" (Revelation 7:9, 12).

"To [God] be glory in the church and in Christ Jesus throughout all generations, forever and ever" (Ephesians 3:21).

 **REFLECTION QUESTIONS**

- Examine all of the various things that you are involved in—schoolwork, sports, activities, job, etc. As you work through each of these, how might it be possible to glorify God in each of these areas?

- From the chapter, can you summarize in your own words the three uses of the word "glory"?

- How might enjoying God be a way in which we glorify God?

- Wherever you live, can you find ways in which God's glory is on display?

- If you are a Christian, how might the truth that you will, one day, no longer have sin, but will be transformed from this earthly journey into your heavenly home bring you comfort?

ABOUT THE AUTHOR

Brian H. Cosby (Ph.D., Australian College of Theology) is senior minister of Wayside Presbyterian Church in Signal Mountain, Tennessee, and visiting professor of church history at Reformed Theological Seminary, Atlanta.

He is the author of a dozen books, including *Uncensored: Daring to Embrace the Entire Bible, Giving Up Gimmicks: Reclaiming Youth Ministry from an Entertainment Culture, God's Story: A Student's Guide to Church History*, and two biographies in the Christian Focus Trailblazers Series—*John Bunyan* and *David Brainerd*.

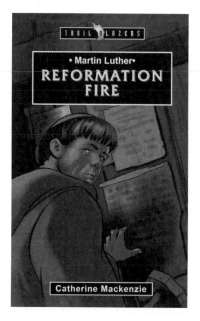

Martin Luther: Reformation Fire
by Catherine Mackenzie
ISBN: 978-1-78191-521-9

What made an ordinary monk become a catalyst for the Reformation in Europe in the 1500s? What were the reasons lying behind his nailing of 95 theses against the practice of indulgences to the door of the Schlosskirche in Wittenberg in 1517? Why was Martin Luther's life in danger? How did his apparent kidnapping result in the first ever New Testament translated into the German language? Discover how a fresh understanding of the Scriptures not only transformed his own life but had a huge impact upon Europe.

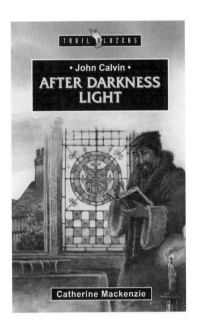

John Calvin: After Darkness Light
by Catherine Mackenzie
ISBN: 978-1-84550-084-9

Calvin had ideas on how we could live better lives – particularly how we could live in close harmony with God and each other – but because his ideas were radical, his life was filled with dramatic events and dangers. He was run out of town – and then welcomed back. He was accused of being too harsh – and also too tender-hearted. When he explained what the Bible meant he was considered too logical and too spiritual! He must have been an amazing man to have caused such a stir!

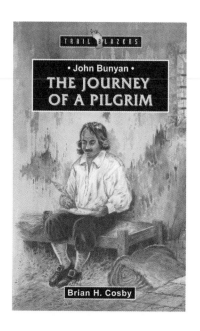

John Bunyan: The Journey of a Pilgrim
by Brian H. Cosby
ISBN: 978-1-84550-458-8

John Bunyan's life was an exciting one. That's what he had wanted as a young man. He had left the security of his father's workshop to join the Parliamentary troops fighting against King Charles. John knows he isn't good enough to get to heaven. But when he realises that Jesus Christ is the only one who is good enough, the real excitement begins. Bunyan's journey takes him through the Civil War and into other conflicts. John Bunyan, the tinker soldier, became one of the world's favourite Christian writers

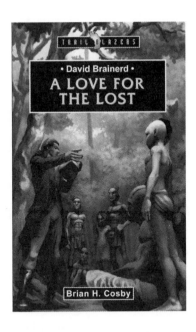

David Brainerd: A Love for the Lost
by Brian H. Cosby
ISBN: 978-1-84550-695-7

Life on the American frontier in the early 1700s was very difficult – continually threatened by disease, attack, and brutally cold winters. The English and Native Americans lived side by side, which often led to conflict. David Brainerd arose as a compassionate and fearless missionary to the various Indian tribes in America. In this book, Brian Cosby takes the reader on a journey from Brainerd's teenage years on the farm to his expulsion from Yale; from preaching on the frontier to his death in his late 20s.

OTHER BOOKS IN THE TRAILBLAZERS SERIES

For a full list of Trailblazers, please see our website:
www.christianfocus.com
All Trailblazers are available as e-books

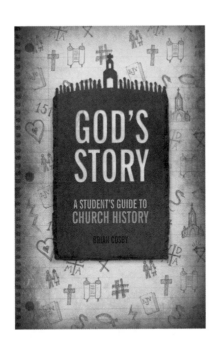

God's Story
A Student's Guide to Church History
by Brian Cosby
ISBN 978-1-78191-320-8

Brian Cosby makes the past come alive for students to explain Christian identity and to help readers avoid past mistakes. The history of the church reveals God's story for the world – despite the sin, corruption, and twisted events in the church's past, God has preserved this remnant, His people. Get a new understanding of His plan for the church and your life.

CHRISTIAN FOCUS PUBLICATIONS

Christian Focus   Christian Heritage   CF4K   Mentor

Christian Focus Publications publishes books for adults and children under its four main imprints: Christian Focus, CF4K, Mentor and Christian Heritage. Our books reflect our conviction that God's Word is reliable and Jesus is the way to know him, and live for ever with him.

Our children's publication list includes a Sunday School curriculum that covers pre-school to early teens, and puzzle and activity books. We also publish personal and family devotional titles, biographies and inspirational stories that children will love.

If you are looking for quality Bible teaching for children then we have an excellent range of Bible stories and age-specific theological books.

From pre-school board books to teenage apologetics, we have it covered!

Find us at our web page:
www.christianfocus.com

CF4 •K
Because you're never too young to know Jesus